Slowly

A Recipe for a
Modern Lifestyle

Kedren Crosby, MPS

WORK WISDOM PRESS

Originally printed in 2009
Reprint © **2021 Kedren Crosby**
All rights reserved.
Designed by Modern Art
ISBN: 978-1-008-94894-5
Imprint: Lulu.com

For my speedy
friends and colleagues
who have been asking
for deceleration advice.

Contents

Introduction

Why I Had To Write This Book

"It's a beautiful day. Don't let it get away.
What you don't have you don't need it now."

U2

WHERE ARE YOU RIGHT NOW? In a hurry somewhere? Do you have that gnawing sensation that maybe there are other things you should be doing? Have any of your phones or computers or PDAs rung or vibrated at you since you opened this book? I want this advice to stick to you, so you need to turn off all of your technology right now. This is shockingly hard, but you need to do it. Be prepared for phantom tremors. Okay? Done? Now, I'm giving you permission to go into a room all by yourself, close the door and make yourself comfortable. That's going to help us to connect. Thanks.

Hopefully you aren't at the end of your real or even perceived rope right now, but if you picked up this book, you must be at least curious about the idea of slowing down. I am hoping that you have not reached the frenetic depths that I did before I chose to live slowly. You may have though, in which case, I'm writing this book just for you, because God knows I couldn't find 'the book' no matter how many times

7

I googled 'slow living...slowly...slow down...slow life...'.

Maybe you actually are being given the opportunity to slow down because of the economy. If you are one of the many souls who have lost their position in an austere job market, you could consider this time in your life as an opportunity to become newly focused on what your ultimate interests are and find joy in living slowly, intentionally, and authentically. Seamus Heaney talks about the 'meeting point of hope and history' where what has happened is met by what we make of it. This break from the rat race may be a gift, after all.

Let me tell you what wild thing happened to me, because maybe it's happening to you, too.

Once upon a time, I had a big-deal job which seemed impossible, bosses who were unrealistic, children who were extremely needy, a million volunteer requests from every school/church/nonprofit in our city, a dirty house, a weedy garden, an unkempt lawn, dirty windows, homework to be overseen, piano practice to supervise and a TO DO list that I refused to enumerate because it was too depressingly long. To boot, there were rarely clean clothes available to put on my children or food in the fridge to pack in lunches—falling miles short of my pipe dream of organic, homegrown, homemade food to nourish my wee ones. Quite honestly, I stopped actually *listening* to people when they talked to me because I was always thinking about my next agenda item. I started experiencing memory problems (because I wasn't actually *experiencing* my life in the first place, so why would I remember it?), joint pain in my hands and feet and I gained 15 pounds. Surprise surprise, red wine didn't help.

In spite of reality, my career was going extraordinarily well. Powerful and smart men were applauding me as an excellent example of a HypoManic Edge woman who could have it all. However, life's icing on the cake—hosting dinner parties, baking bread, sending birthday cards, reading books, researching new ideas, the *New York Times Book Review*, spontaneous chats with friends—were totally out of the question. I felt like I couldn't even keep the basics of life together, so there was completely no way I had time for niceties. I needed more than a day at the spa to take me away from that grim reality.

A few frenetic years into this pace, I freaked out at work. Oh, I *thought* it was a perfectly valid melt down—something about contracts and regulations and 'perceived public perception' of the organization of which I was C.E.O. I urgently texted my attorney friend in ALL CAPS with lots of expletives and red explanation marks (&(Q^#$) Q!!!!!!! to convey the desperate nature of the situation and that I was at the end of my (#Q^$*#^* rope!!! Now, you must know that this friend is older, wiser, hipper and works for people who are truly TRULY at the end of their rope. Many long and frantic hours later, I received a one-word, underlined email back from him, **"CALMATE!!"**

I had to look it up on www.urbandictionary.com. Through the tears I cracked up laughing and recognized the truth in his solitary word. I desperately need to CALMATE.

I am an Introvert Intuitive Thinking Judger (INTJ) on my Meyers-Briggs personality profile; a Type A over-achiever with two graduate degrees and four fixer-upper-houses under my belt. I was a world-renowned Spazmatologist. I had absolutely no training in how to CALMATE, or even how to slow down long enough to gage my own sense of imbalance. Like most of Americans, I was taught how to make goals and pursue them. Period. I was never taught how to check in with one's own emotions, needs, wants. God knows that I certainly never *ever* learned how to sit still and just observe my thoughts.

Once I was clear on my diagnosis (living too fast), I sought a remedy. There was simply no book or website that offered me a solution, but over the years I have pieced together many different sources, people, ideas and disciplines that I concocted into a recipe that has transformed my life into the most beautiful experience I could ever ask for. *I'm actually happy, and it's nobody's doing but my own. You can be happy, too, through your own doing and non-doing.*

What's ironic is that I absolutely should have known better than to jump so willingly onto the self-perpetuating gerbil wheel. I had followed the Slow Food movement for over a decade. I had killed my television in the late 80s. I chose to move to Lancaster, PA because I fell in love with the idea of creating an authentic life in a Slow City. I even walked to work. I forayed into designing a good life when I worked in an AIDS housing program in Baltimore. After spending my time trying to provide residents with what was commonly referred to as a "good death", I began my list of what constitutes a *good* **life**'. I spent time with men and women who were dying, heard their stories and decided that I wanted live so well, so fully, so honestly that I would be at peace on my deathbed. I'd studied all about *Bowling Alone* and even taught a version of *Getting to Yes*, but I still didn't know how to 'calmate' when it came down to daily living. I needed to figure out how to incorporate the concept of living slowly at a more cellular level, so that it radiated into all parts of my life. I needed some slow principles to lead me.

This may seem too simplistic, but there is no value in complicating matters: I started seeing my life as a recipe and my daily activities as the ingredients. My life could be repulsive (and I'd already burned that casserole) or quite tasty, but it all depended on what ingredients went into the daily mixing bowl. Since I was the only one who selected the ingredients, there was no reason why I couldn't just change the ingredients and enjoy a delicious dish of a life.

It isn't just YOUR life that benefits from living slowly. The people you love as well as those you don't even like will bloom in your presence once you start living slowly. People you don't know will benefit from your new pace. Your grandchildren's grandchildren will thank you. It's sort of magical, except that it's not a mystery. It's just a recipe.

We all are hard-wired to live at different speeds and we all start this process at various levels of awareness about what we need and how to get it. The path will be different for each of us, as are the outcomes. Comparing your experience with someone else's will not help. Each of us has a unique life and we wouldn't want someone else's: our own life can be amazing because we get to design it and live it according to exactly what we like best. We get to design our own life, tailor-made to suit our preferences. This is so lucky!

There are some extremely healthy, tasty, energizing ingredients I consider essential to a life so luscious you want to savor it. These ingredients help me to slow down and actually *PAY ATTENTION* so I can live a good and memorable life. I've included descriptions of these ingredients in Chapter Four of this book. If you feel you've been bitten by a 'too fast' life and the poison is moving toward your heart, these are the antidotes. Of course, you need to slow down long enough to figure out what your instincts, your body, your mind and your 'taste buds' are telling you that you need.

Recall from kindergarten that every snowflake is unique and each of us is just as special too, right? Because we are all different, your recipe needs to be tailored to include your unique proportions of the essential ingredients. These amounts will change over time. You have to pay attention to yourself every day. It's absolutely critical to learn how to listen to yourself for the rest of your life and figure out how to 'season to taste' this recipe! I am so happy to share the essential components, but the appropriate amounts of each item can only be determined by you.

Living Slowly has made me a different person, and many overwhelmed folks have been asking me all about the Kool-aid I've been drinking and where they can get their hands on some. A few months ago, my friend and former colleague from Baltimore emailed me with a desperate plea for help. "Mary" is a smart 30-something: a funny, gorgeous, talented whippersnapper who, like so many of the people I love, was waking up after lousy sleep to find herself overwhelmed, crazed and feeling as if she also held a graduate degree in Spazmatology. She was growing into adulthood and accumulating so many roles that she was beginning to begrudge her new house, her husband, her job, her volunteer work, her city and even her friends. Just as I experienced, she was gaining weight, drinking too much and getting irritable with everyone. The house, husband, city, body-image, friends and family were all sources of joy prior to the pile of responsibilities towering too high. She had some brilliant instincts about a course of action to turn the ship around, but she needed affirmation. She only knew the mini 'Christmas Card Version" of my personal slow revolution, but she wanted advice on how to start living more intentionally. I felt like the older, wiser sister in a Jane Austen adaptation.

Does this sound like anyone you know? Mary is just one of many, many of my friends and colleagues who are increasingly exhausted, overwhelmed, unconnected to the community, distanced from their lovers, depressed and anxiety-ridden. And they are all amazing people—people who have capacity for great joy! Unlike the pharmaceutical industry which is quick to offer a prescription, I'd like to think that some of these problems can be resolved by replicating the behaviors of people who have remained balanced and happy in spite of their jobs, blackberries, commutes, families and overwhelming responsibilities.

Mary's S.O.S. triggered a series of calls and emails, where we identified her ultimate interests. We talked about new ingredients she could incorporate into her life which would help her accomplish her true goals and become her best, most balanced self without sacrificing anything she considered a valued priority. The life changes came, along with peace and happiness. It took brutal honesty, loving kindness, faith, elbow-grease and sacrifice (repeat after me, 'sacrifice is not a dirty word, sacrifice is not a dirty word'). This is a grown-up, authentic, sustainable way of building your own dolce vita. It worked out beautifully for her, and for me, too. I'm not suggesting that our windows are squeaky clean or the laundry is always folded or we've become wealthy or we are no longer aging. But, we have found happiness and peace and there is nothing nicer than that.

I owe this now beautiful life of mine to several wise men and women who saw how very far down the 'shallow-hole' I had fallen and shared with me their unconventional methods for clawing my way out. This book can be your rope, but you need to do the climbing.

Life is short. Savor it.

1

What is Living Slowly?

"When you walk, walk; when you eat, eat;
and when you sit, sit."

ZEN KOAN

LIVING SLOWLY IS PACING YOUR LIFE at a speed which allows you to pay close attention to those things you value most in the long-term.

When you live at the right pace and wholly experience your life, you savor small kindnesses, gestures, words, portions, gifts and loves. There is no 'pressure cooker' anxiety in living slowly. You will appreciate little and big life lessons, too.

Living slowly allows you to live sparsely and simply. You don't need to consume too much because you will be aware, appreciative and satisfied with smaller amounts. This is how living slowly facilitates the slimming of your environmental footprint. You won't want the McMansion, the Hummer or the Big Gulp. If you live slowly, you will find that you enjoy every square inch of your life and you wouldn't dream of wanting more than you need.

An Idea Whose Time Has Come

"Barn's burnt down –Now I can see the moon."

MASAHIDE (17TH CENTURY JAPANESE POET)

I USED TO HAVE GRADUATE STUDENTS to compile data for me. I would send them off to census.gov to produce statistics. Today, I have neither students or figures at my fingertips. Honestly, I am not concerned about precise numbers, as they will be different tomorrow. It is worthwhile, however, to think about these indicators. Even without exact numbers, we know Americans are struggling.

- Obesity rates are _____.

- The average American meal takes _____ minutes to consume.

- _____% of Americans are suffering from diabetes.

- The average adult in America has $_____ in personal debt.

- _____% of Americans filed for bankruptcy last year.

- The average American creates ___tons of garbage.

Let's be honest with ourselves without being judgmental.

- The average American occupies _____ number of square feet.

- The average environmental footprint of an American would require us to have ___ planet earths if everyone lived this decadently.

- The average American drives _____ miles per year.

- The average American has ____ pairs of shoes.

- The average American trades in their car with _____miles on it.

- The average American adult has meaningful sex ___ time per year.

- _____% of the adult population engages in volunteer work.

- Adult Americans attend an average of _____ dinner parties/picnics/cocktail parties a year.

- ___% of adult Americans report being depressed or unhappy.

- ___% of adult Americans have a prescription for antidepressants or anti-anxiety medication.

- The average American spends ___# of hours per day in front of a screen.

Let's be honest with ourselves without being judgmental. If we knew these numbers, they wouldn't be pretty. We got here because of our behavior. We behaved that way for a reason.

Walk yourself through the indicators above and consider what your personal statistics might look like? Don't judge it, but do own it.

Now that the barn's burnt down, we can look for the moon!

3

Who Benefits from your Living Slowly?

"The most consummately beautiful thing in the universe is the rightly fashioned life of a good person."

GEORGE HERBERT PALMER

You benefit, most of all.

You will truly find the change within yourself miraculous when you begin living slowly. As with any 'before and after' pictures, the transformation is most dramatic for those who were an utter catastrophe 'before'. If you are currently a Hypomanic or on the verge of complete burnout, your 'after' picture will be unrecognizable. Adopting the Essential Ingredients in Chapter Four will seem to reconfigure you at the cellular level. I am elated every time I encounter a former colleague who invariably says, "Is that you, Kedren? You seem like a completely different person." Amen to that!

The more you incorporate these ingredients into your life, the more you will find yourself to be open, grateful, kind and warm-hearted. Externally, you may find yourself thinner, less apt to escape to your demons, financially healthier and less cluttered. You will glow knowing that your imprint on the earth decreases as you want and consume less. As you pay attention and make adjustments accordingly, you will be giddy with the results of this extreme inside-out makeover.

Your family benefits now and for future generations

Your family will reap enormous and lasting benefits from your new lifestyle. At first, they may be in shock as you begin making choices to live more slowly, but they will blossom once they have your full attention. They will also enjoy being with a calm, sane, humble person rather than a frenzied one who finds drama at every corner. Holidays and vacations are more fun even though they may be less expensive. Clothes are cleaner even though they are older. The empty spaces provide opportunities for incidental learning that happens almost effortlessly.

It's a cinch to convey our beliefs because the kids are there at the peace marches, the yoga classes, the women's conferences and church, too. Jackie Kennedy said, "If you bungle raising your children, I don't think whatever else you do matters very much." If I'm bungling now, at least it isn't for lack of attention to the relationship.

I asked my family if they felt they have benefited from our deceleration. These are the results:

Tess, my 8 year old: *"Love is the strongest weapon we have in the world and you are using it."* Whoa. Also from Tess, *"You help us with our homework now. You realized that we needed to change schools, too."*

Tommie, my 9 year old: *"I like that you cook now. And you don't cry anymore. I wish you would let us get out of bed more slowly though."* Comedian, that one.

My parents appreciate that I am less short-tempered. I visit more often. My cousins, in-laws and grandmother had assumed I had been eaten by wolves during those many years when I was otherwise preoccupied. Now, they get cards and the occasional gift or baked goods. These little kindnesses previously ranked so low on my TO DO list that they never happened. I felt pretty lousy that I couldn't get them to happen, too.

In considering the benefits to our families and our earth, it is useful to consider the Indigenous American standards for assessing tribe decision-making. They felt that the present generation was obligated to contribute to the well-being of future generations, most especially the well-being of the seventh generation. God knows that I won't be endowing any trust funds to my grandchildren, but I hope that my practice of living slowly trickles down in some beneficial way to future generations of my people.

People you know in your community will benefit

Both times I attended graduate schools in Baltimore, I was assigned chapters from Robert Putnum's **Bowling Alone.** Dr. Putnum visited Lancaster to speak at Franklin and Marshall College in March, 2004. It was free to the public, so I was there, front and center, cheering him on as if he were Bono. He gave us a homework assignment that night which I have taken to heart: find ways to increase social capital in America.

Social Capital is a concept developed in sociology that refers to connections within and across social networks, as well as connections among individuals. The idea is that social networks have value. Just as a screwdriver (physical capital) or a college education (human capital) can increase productivity, so too can social contacts affect the productivity of individuals and groups.

There are many kinds of social capital; informal (dinner parties, picnics, volunteering at a school) or formal (churches, clubs, boards of directors). There is *Bridge Social Capital*—where you make connections across diverse, unconnected groups of people – like at jury duty. There is also *Bond Social Capital*, where you connect with people who are similar to you—like at a country club, church or peace march.

When you slow down, you will likely feel more enthusiastic about building social capital. You will have enough energy left in your personal stores to share a little bit of yourself with others. When I was living in the fast lane, I didn't feel that I had time to invite people into my house. How could I possibly have a dinner party when the laundry was piled on the dining room table waiting to be folded? Now that I'm living slowly, I have become very selective about how I spend time in my community. As part of the deceleration process, I had to unplug from some social networks and become my own ruthless gatekeeper. However, I'm more loving and attentive when I do choose to spend time with people. I am also more engaged when I am at the party/board meeting/school playground/work event. Just as it is in the realms of food and material possessions, slow social capital requires choosing high quality, small portions over gluttonous quantities of lesser quality.

There are many categories of people in the community that may benefit as a result of your choosing to live slowly. The friendships you decide to nurture will blossom as you become more attentive and less self-absorbed. The neighbors will appreciate your stopping to hold a conversation, perhaps even dinner parties or neighborhood potlucks or block parties. You may find you have the energy to develop friendly relationships with local merchants and the stand holders at your farmers market.

There is power in your decision to purchase products that are local, authentic, well-crafted and cruelty-free. It's helpful to think of this less as sacrifice than as a reorganization of how you use your time and resources. It's a zero sum game, and there will be more of you left if you give up some of the empty calories in your life. If you choose to volunteer at a school, the staff will benefit from your help, as will the children. A nonprofit that is near and dear to your heart might be a worthwhile use of your passion, and the staff there will benefit from your engagement. Perhaps you will start feeding your spirituality, in which case, your addition to that community will be beneficial. Maybe you will take a class? Know that your intentional energy will benefit these neighbors, businesses, children, clients, staff, boards, faculty and fellow learners. They will be so glad that you chose to play a small role in their lives.

People that you don't even know in your community will benefit
Other beneficiaries are less obvious. A friend just spent a month in Mexico and gave a private viewing of her slides. I was flabbergasted by all of the beautiful public decorations in the streets. I asked if the government hired artists to create and install all of the gorgeous eye candy and she said, "Oh no, it's just the abuelas in the town that feel compelled to make the town beautiful. They just do it." These women are living slowly enough to have energy to make beauty for people that they don't even know. It's breathtaking on several levels, isn't it?

When I was a new mother of 'Irish twins' (born one year apart), I was having a heck of a time keeping all the balls in the air. Honestly, the friendly playgrounds in Lancaster City saved my sanity on more than one occasion. Playgrounds are stellar opportunities for social capital with strangers. The parents, grandparents and children that I would meet often felt like little gifts. Just a bit of small talk or shared experience helped me feel ground beneath my feet, even when there wasn't any.

The parks, markets and sidewalks in our daily lives provide opportunities to rebuild our respect for strangers and the community in which we live. The small smiles exchanged with people unlike you are extremely valuable because they make all of us recognize our connectedness. Establishing a quiet, non-committed relationship with people we don't actually know helps us feel positive about our communities and even humankind. It makes us a kinder society. We begin to think twice about regressive social policy when we literally and figuratively rub shoulders with rich and poor, white and Black, young and old, every day. Again, this is a concept that seems so simple and perhaps old-fashioned, but it has such power. Experiment and notice. It is jet fuel for peace on earth and goodwill toward humankind.

Consider your own examples as you walk through your day with your eyes wide opened. What makes you feel hope? The old man at the grocery store who tells me that he likes my hat restores my belief that humankind is generous. The young mother who stops to love up my dog gives me pride in my community. The gorgeous flirt at the market who holds the door for me makes me feel alive. This is a gentle way to create a hopeful revolution.

Jane Jacobs writes about the natural beauty of the 'sidewalk ballet' in *The Death and Life of Great American Cities.* Robert Putnum asserts in Bowling Alone that, since the decline in social capital began in 1964, Americans have become increasingly disconnected which in turn causes distrust, ill-health and loneliness. I buy every word he says because I lived it. Amitai Etzioni, the father of Communitarianism, asserts that yes, we do have rights as individuals, but we also have responsibilities to our community. America is the ultimate individualist society, and perhaps this makes us have an especially difficult time taking care of the responsibilities to the community. It's fascinating to think about how far we could rebuild strong villages through living slowly. It's this fascia, in between the joints, where happy communities grow. Slowing down allows us to build fuller lives with strangers through small gestures and hopeful connections.

The earth benefits

Simply by becoming more intentional, you will find that you will want less. The more you pay attention to the present moment, thing or person, the less you feel compelled to cram in more moments, things and people. By consuming less, the earth benefits. When you are living slowly, you will likely consume less processed food, so there will be less need for fertilizer and toxic runoff from animal waste. The ground, the water and the ozone layer all will benefit. You won't feel as compelled to keep up with the latest trends as you learn to adopt sustainable style and simplicity, so there will be fewer cars, clothes, gadgets and home décor ending up in landfills. Mother Earth will thank you.

Nourishing Wisdom is a mind-body nutrition book by Marc David and something of a movement, too. My yoga pals who adhere to this way of eating have explained to me that you truly have more energy when you consume less food. I think this concept can be expanded to recognize that you gain more energy from less consumption of many kinds. This can be taken to an extreme, but don't be extreme! Listen closely to your perceived versus real needs and be cognizant of what you are putting into your mouth, your home, your storage unit. You don't want to take in more than you need. Somewhere on the earth there will be a deficit if you are taking more than your fair share. Insatiable is not sustainable.

You may find great pleasure in reducing your environmental footprint. If that is part of your recipe for living slowly, you may find yourself choosing veganism, buying organic and green products, growing a victory garden and living in the community where you work and play. You will begin repairing your clothes and shoes and delaying the purchase of new ones until you truly need them. Maybe you choose to self-propel to work or you just choose to keep your car until it eventually dies. Regardless of how deeply you venture into greening, living slowly allows you to consider your consumption's impact on the earth and provides the time you need to change hurtful behaviors.

Eyes wide open disclaimer

There may be those who do not feel they are benefiting from your new lifestyle. You may have friends whom you find to be toxic. You need to honestly explain to them that you are going to be focusing on a few priorities and, as a result, you will be less available. While it is uncomfortable, it is necessary to minimize interaction with people

Seeds of discontent cannot grow in a grateful heart.

who lead you down your slippery slopes. You know who they are. They may feel they aren't benefiting from your new lifestyle because they will see you less. You are actually providing an excellent role model for them in the event they eventually choose to live more intentionally or authentically.

Some of us have found we needed to work in conventional jobs less in order to live slowly. There will be colleagues and community members who cannot understand why you would decelerate when you are at the top of your game. You may be told you are committing career suicide or lose your place in the social caste system. These colleagues may not recognize how they are benefiting from your counter cultural move. You need to take care of yourself. You only have one life. You may be surprised by how many high-profile people will tell you that they fantasize about slowing down but they have big buts. (In the movie *Pee Wee's Big Adventure*, Pee Wee Herman attempts to convince his friend to take a risk. She's afraid to do it and stutters to Pee Wee, "But, but but, but…" Finally Pee Wee assures her to take the risk by telling her, "Everybody's got a big but!"). Don't have a big but!

Your family may have grown accustomed to microwaves and screens. They may throw a coup d'état if you tell them that you are going to work part-time, fire the nanny, sit on a meditation pillow and skip this year's trip to Disney World. Only you know how to change the behavior of your own complex family. Journaling and the "How to Talk" books by Faber and Mazlish might help you find some solutions. I know that at our nightly sit-down dinners, we always make a point of going around the table and sharing why we are grateful. Seeds of discontent cannot grow in a grateful heart.

4

Slow Cooking Your Dolce Vida

The Essential Ingredients

IN ADDITION TO THE ESSENTIAL INGREDIENTS described in this chapter, your recipe will be tastier if you incorporate the ten tenets below into your methods. Most importantly, remember that you must season to taste! You alone are the sole chef regarding the optimal ratios of ingredients.

This is not warfare on Fast. To declare war on anything is to strengthen its power. Listen closely to your words and thoughts. Beware of becoming ANTI-fast.

This cannot be about DEPRIVATION. It's not a diet or a budget or Lent. It's not about martyrdom, it's about reframing your wants and recognizing what you truly need. It's about reorganizing how you spend your energy, time, love and money so that you have enough and even a little extra to spread around. It's almost indulgent, but only in a select few areas. You choose those areas in which you treat yourself.

Go toward those things that give you and your loved ones peace. Go toward what makes you feel whole and away from what feels vacuous.

Of course, this necessitates taking the time to uncover what makes you feel most balanced in the long run.

Incrementally tweak your life by adding more of the essential ingredients. Mull these over. Chew. Do not make any sudden moves.

Examine your unhealthy actions without judgment. Name them, bring them into the light and consider them with curiosity and loving kindness. Ask WHY over and over and peel back the onion of your unfulfilling behaviors. Let the vapid, fast, shallow, temporary behaviors lose their seductive qualities over time. Wear them down by seeing them for the false friends they are. Let them lose their illicitness. This is how to create lasting behavior change.

Accept that everyone's recipe for their dolce vita will look different when it's done. Everyone needs different things. Your ideal recipe may change from year to year as you evolve. In the same vein, you cannot judge another's recipe if it is working well for them. We are all unique with different tastes and needs. Don't compare your trip to others' journeys. There is no point!

Fast livers may be suspicious of you—even belittle you perhaps. Stop. See it. Let it happen. Let it go.

Don't regret your past. One must travel through chaos in order to find real peace.

The more you wake up to what's ultimately important, the more you will find that your need for speed, status and materialism will wear away. You will need to run to these false friends less often because you won't want to escape.

You may occasionally miss your old, chaotic, dramatic life. Recognize that you can have drama or you can have peace. You cannot have both. Choose peace most of the time.

Self-Examination

*"The moment one gives close attention to anything,
even a blade of grass, it becomes a mysterious, awesome,
indescribably magnificent world in itself."*

HENRY MILLER

HONESTLY PAY ATTENTION TO YOURSELF. Honestly. Pay attention. To yourself.

Self-examination is the foundation for living slowly. If this recipe was for soup, self-examination would be the broth. The other ingredients can be folded in according to your preferences but they must absolutely float around in a nourishing liquid of authentic self-examination.

Being courageously honest with yourself is the first step. It may take brute strength to refute some of the lies you have been retelling yourself throughout your entire life. In trying to examine yourself, you may want to assume the role of an outside investigator. Why would she do that action—over and over. *Why?* You may need to pretend to be a third party watching with curiosity, kindness and extreme acuity. *Why?*

You will only be able to live intentionally if you are willing to ask yourself the hard questions. In the midst of things falling apart, you can ask yourself "Why did this happen? Honestly, what role did I play? What lesson is to be learned from this mess? What is my responsibility here?" Whether it is the reality of your enormous debt, the horror of a child's failing report card or the slow demise of an important relationship, there is an opportunity to sit with this reality and learn from it. One must slow down enough to allow the honesty to seep in. You will need to have both courage and empty spaces in order to take off the rose-colored glasses and see what truly is. When you discover your true self, you will be able to more accurately assess your needs and wants. You will be more likely to determine where you are stuck, what the obstacles are to loving more fully and living with more kindness and less materialism.

Authentic self-examination also enables you to hone your instincts. These instincts help to calibrate how fast or slow you need to move and recognize your tendencies. You will begin to recognize unhealthy patterns you create for yourself, over and over. This authentic self-examination will allow you to evolve by giving you the necessary self-knowledge to eventually begin changing your behavior.

My brutally honest, curious and loving self-examination has taught me extraordinary lessons. Whereas I used to view myself as a victim, now I can see unhealthy tendencies toward paranoia. I used to think my career and salary defined my value. Now I think I'm worthwhile because I work hard to enhance a few key lives and add love into my community. I used to perform articulate, angry, educated, rather entertaining rants about politics and injustice. They made me feel righteous and smart. Now I recognize that was my ego puffing up to be noticed, and that it is more valuable to take the offender out for lunch and speak in soft words. I used to crave attention from many powerful people. Now I realize that I had lacked a sense of self-worth that I was seeking to fill in an unsustainable way. I was emotionally unavailable. Now I recognize that I didn't want to let them see hidden parts of my life. I used to drink and eat too much in an attempt to fill a heart-hole of loneliness. Now I recognize that being alone is not something I want to eradicate. I rather like being with me, as I am sometimes funny and cozy company. Your discernment will likely result in different realizations than mine because your issues and motivations are unique. The point is, once you see what is really happening and dissect and demystify the fictitious stories you tell yourself, you can eventually make changes more readily.

I have four suggested methods for authentic self-examination. These have effectively helped me to drill down to my true self.

Morning Pages

Far and away, the most effective means for my continuous self-examination is through journaling Morning Pages. Using the Julia Cameron method described in *The Artist's Way,* I try to handwrite three pages of stream of consciousness journaling every day. Magically, miraculously, themes pop up, issues reveal themselves and solutions are tucked in between the scrawls. Without morning pages, I would not be able to concretely identify my greatest obstacles to growth. Buy her book, read her directions and start tomorrow morning. Morning Pages are an exceptional barometer for measuring the health of one's life. Morning Pages are both diagnostic and therapeutic.

Therapy

Therapy can be jet-fuel for your evolution, but the right therapist is critical. Ask friends who are like-minded if they have any recommendations. When you meet with a therapist, tell them you would like to start with a trial period of two months. At the end of that period, talk together to decide if you should continue or find another therapist. Also, therapy simply will not work at all if you are not honest and complete with your words. Tell them the truth! Be naked (figuratively)! Just like your medical doctor, they have seen it all before. Nothing is going to surprise them. If you simply are telling the therapist lies, it will be impossible for them to help you discern solutions.

Meditation

Meditation may seem a bit unconventional, but it is so incredibly effective that it is wise for you to get over your discomfort with any freaky-deaky conceptions you have of this important tool. Perhaps you can call it 'praying' or 'alone time' if those words feel more comfortable. Meditation is actually about *not* thinking, but somehow, it provides the space for one's brain to make leaps in evolution. Meditation connects the brain with the body, which is so rare in our time. Our brains are almost always being fed with our iPods, cell phones, computers, tvs or stereos, so meditation gives our consciousness a chance to finally be heard. Our spirits are so often solely on the receiving end of communication. Meditation allows them a chance to be heard. It has so many good things to say, if only we take some time to listen.

I was first taught to meditate during a yoga class using a very simple mantra. We just sat on the floor, eyes open looking forward, and repeated this inside of our heads, in sync with our breathing..."

"May I be happy.
May I be healthy.
May I be free from danger.
May I have ease of well-being."

I recall very clearly that first time, sitting artificially still, with my watery eyes pinned to a dirt smear on the wall, "I have none of these things." After two years of living slowly, I find that I have all of these things.

The self-examination component of meditation reveals itself like gentle little captions bubbling up from these lines in the mantra. Often after a deep inhale of 'may I be happy', a little soap bubble grows and the words inside it say something like "write your grandmother". It doesn't happen every time, but it happens more often now that I am comfortable with my meditation practice. Along with the exhale on 'May I be healthy' there may be the thought "eat some spinach". I can't explain it without sounding, in fact, freaky deaky, because it seems as if my subconscious is actually suggesting ways for me to be all these things. It's just the way it works. There are a million ways to meditate, find a simple one you like and try it for a couple of weeks.

Research your issues

Another tool for concocting a delectable broth of self-examination is by reading books on the issues that reveal themselves in your Morning Pages, Therapy and Meditation practices. Once an issue presents itself, just go to the library, online or to the bookstore and look at what relevant literature exists. Borrow or buy the book if you think it is going to help you evolve. For example, I needed heavy doses of Leo Buscaglia and M. Scott Peck to help me to the other shore. They are on the top shelf of my bedside bookshelf and never ever get dusty.

You may not need to employ all of these methods. However, you may. These tools lay down some salt and gravel to mitigate the slippery slopes of fast times, egoism, materialism, imbalanced technology, loneliness and a whole host of addictions. Use these tools to become more of your wondrous true self and turn to them quickly when you notice that you are veering off the rails.

Boundaries

"Why do I give valuable time to people who don't care if I live or if I die?"

THE SMITHS

IN ORDER TO CLEAR some space in your life for newfound deliciousness, you must eliminate some existing unpalatable clutter. Time is a zero sum game, so you will need to rearrange your energy expenditures. Personally, I found a great deal of low-hanging fruit in defining new boundaries. By learning how to manage my energy using boundaries, I've eliminated a huge amount of counterproductive waste.

Based on the first thirty some years of my life, it just might seem that there is simply no living creature less qualified to discuss boundaries. Much of the past mess in my life is owing to the fact that I was born with a congenital deformity—lacking that invisible force field that most humans use to both protect themselves and to cautiously not venture too far into another person's world. I have had to learn how to create boundaries on my own as an adult. So, from a more positive perspective, I am quite well qualified since I have had to learn how to build this amorphous second skin at the quantum level. It is critically important that one develop healthy boundaries in order to live slowly. The destruction and time-suck due to poor boundaries can absolutely destroy your efforts to live a happy, intentional life. If you don't have any or your boundaries are too permeable, I suggest that you nurture strong yet porous boundaries of your own.

Boundaries have two aspects—they are both protective and assertive. First, they serve to protect you by what I imagine looks like a thick layer of translucent goo pulsing several inches outside of your body. It's like another layer of skin—alive and pulsing. This boundary can sense when a creepy, personality disordered or hateful person is in your midst. Effective protective boundaries quickly harden and repel the energies of such destructive characters to make it impossible for them to get under your skin. If you don't have protective boundaries, ruinous people will be drawn to you like sweaty children to the ice cream truck.

Boundaries also allow one to know the appropriate distance you should travel into another person's space. I call these assertive boundaries. They push out from your body and get close to another person. If your assertive boundaries are too aggressive, they will not recognize the socially acceptable distances and venture in too close. I'm not necessarily talking about physically too close, but emotionally too close. This will confuse other people. People with well-functioning boundaries won't know if you are presenting yourself as just a friend or a potential BFF or even lover. They won't be able to discern when you are simply an employee or if you are a drinking buddy. This will sometimes excite them. They will call you 'a breath of fresh air,' but the reality is that this usually ends in gnashing of teeth on both sides of the confusion.

I suggest that you examine how healthy both your protective and assertive boundaries are. Ask yourself some of these questions and journal your answers.

Do you often feel used?

Do you spend free time with people who don't care about you?

Do you get sucked in to activities that you don't really care about?

Do people flirt with you?

Do you often later regret things you've said?

Do you have awkwardness with colleagues or friends because they don't know how to treat you?

Boundaries with people

I had many, many people in my life before I decelerated. For a wide variety of reasons, some of those folks were not good traveling companions on the journey toward a more intentional life. They couldn't aid in propelling me toward a life that was going to value kindness, love, forgiveness and voluntary simplicity.

In learning boundaries, I had to become my own ruthless gatekeeper. Just as a politician's Chief of Staff is diligent in keeping time-wasters out of their boss's office and email inbox, you must become your own ruthless gatekeeper. You must figure out what you want your friends' characteristics to be and then stick to that list of criteria as you begin weeding and cultivating your beautiful garden of companions. In order to be a good gatekeeper for yourself, you need to establish what you want your companions to be like. Here is my personal list:

The characteristics of Kedren's travel companions:

Kind
Forgiving
Happy
Enlightened
Not a whiner
Not a mooch
Not a victim or a blamer
Creative
Funny
Energetic but selective about activities
Open-minded

Soon after I established this list, I was able to recognize the mismatch I had with past friends and acquaintances. I had vampires in my world who would suck energy right out of my body when I was with them. The list showed me in black and white that they just didn't match the job description. No harm, no foul—it was just a bad fit. They weren't the kind of people I needed in my life. Obviously, there are exceptions, but this helps clarify who can give you energy and who will steal it.

Make a list here of some of the characteristics of the *people* you want to populate your new more intentional world.

1.

2.

3.

4.

5.

6.

7.

8.

9.

10.

Friendship

If some person in your life does not exhibit the characteristics of the kind of friends you need in your new life, you need to create a different relationship with them. You may need to journal about this or talk to a therapist depending on the history and connectivity you had with this person. This can run the gamut from 'breaking up' entirely with a particularly toxic person to altering the frequency and intensity of a friendship. Conversely, you may find that you want to move toward certain friends in a more concerted effort if they are a positive source of energy for you.

One of my oldest friends is a heavy drinker and smoker. I can't behave that way because I always end up feeling lousy for days afterward. Once I figured out that spending time with this friend was consistently a slippery slope into decadence, regret and embarrassment, I decided to change the nature of the friendship. I started by telling him how much I loved him, but that I couldn't spend nights at dance clubs and karaoking until 3am. Now, we have lunch or coffee dates and I adore him more than ever for respecting me.

Family

When dealing with in-laws, it is almost always a good idea to have the blood relative negotiate any boundary that is the slightest bit complicated. You will need to be crystal clear with your partner regarding your opinions and goals for the desired outcome. Be sensitive that your partner will want to please everyone, and forgive readily if you don't win.

Romance

One of my married, female friends who is wildly gorgeous and witty has a golden rule for herself when it comes to men. "I don't do lunches. I don't do dinners. And I CERTAINLY don't do drinks." Can you imagine how much heartache would be prevented if everyone adhered to those boundaries? A few of my friends recently decided that their self-imposed FaceBook rule was that they would NOT 'friend' old boyfriends who were serious or for whom they had lingering 'dangerous' feelings.

If you feel that the timing, personalities and connection is right for love, you will need to be open to it. You still need to be clear and articulate to the potential lover about your boundaries although the impulse is to forgo them entirely. Explain to your new beloved those times and places where you have your priorities and request that they respect these values of yours. Maybe you need to have your own quiet time every day? Maybe you don't drink. Maybe you need to have your own religion or group of friends that are not shared with the love interest. Maybe you have a hobby that you would prefer not to share with them. The key is making certain that you both know where they are welcome in your life and where they should not attempt to enter.

Boundaries around how you spend your time

You can also save an enormous amount of time, money and energy if you clearly establish boundaries regarding how you want to spend your time.

First, it's wise to consider how you currently spend your day in the order of time allocated to each activity. I won't mention names, but I know someone whose list looks like this.

Sleeping
Shopping
Drinking
Self-care
Social media
Working
Dating
Talking on the phone
Looking through magazines
Planning vacations

Now, it's your turn to list how you currently spend your time. Remember to be courageously honest.

1.

2.

3.

4.

5.

6.

7.

8.

9.

10.

Take a look at this list you've just drafted. How do you feel about this?

What would you like to delete from the list?

How could you make that happen?

In your new, slower life, what will be the top five activities you want to do with your limited time. List these here.

1.

2.

3.

4.

5.

Communicating boundaries

Just like with a good Chief of Staff, you need to become an effective but *inoffensive* gatekeeper. Be crystal clear and brief. In order to exert healthy boundaries, you need to say the right words in the right tone.

If someone is asking you to get involved in some activity that doesn't fall within your priority activities, you need to learn how to say no. I am often asked to attend fundraisers or join Boards of Directors for nonprofit organizations. Perhaps, given infinite time and resources, I would support them all. But, given my reality, I needed to learn how to decline without burning bridges. It's most effective to do this in a manner that leaves no door open so that the solicitor need not waste their breath or time.

If you just can't say no, I've drafted some scripts for you below:

Drawing the boundary

Whether you are drawing boundaries with people, money or how you choose to spend your time, there are basically four levels of engagement. Figure out which of the four categories is appropriate before communicating this clearly to the relevant party.

❶ Unequivocal NO

It's best to be honest and direct. I think it is kindest to be frank. "No thank you." You don't have to offer any explanation, either.

❷ Conditional NO

"No, I can't do this now/have this relationship now, but I can consider it if a certain circumstance changes."

❸ Yes but later

"Yes, but not until some specific time in the future (when my kids go to school full-time, when I finish some project...). Call me in six months."

❸ Yes and now

"Yes! How can I get started? Here is what I can bring to the table and here is what I can't offer, but I want to be involved."

Requests for money that you would rather not give

"Thank you so much for thinking of me! I think the world of your efforts and your mission. I won't be able to attend this year, but I wish you the best of luck with your event." (if they continue to push the issue, you can just say, "Best of luck, really! I'm sure it will be terrific!")

Requests for your time that you would rather not spend

"I'm so honored that you would like me to be involved! You may have heard that I've been reprioritizing my activities this year. I'm focusing on (insert your top priority here....Your family? Your health? Your writing? Your new career? Your house? Your self-growth?) right now. I won't be able to help with your activity, but I wish you the best. (if you think fast, you might be able to think of some way you could help that also fits your priorities...I tend to offer to drop off a baked good—this way I can spend time baking with my kids but don't need to be away from them).

Requests for your emotions that you would rather not expend
"As you know, I'm working very hard on focusing on a few priorities right now. I don't have the energy to invest in this relationship."

Learning how to assert healthy boundaries aligned with your priorities will free up a great deal of your time, money and energy, too. I urge you to spend time considering your ultimate goals as well as strategies for building fences around those precious priorities to keep them safe.

Want Less

"I've learned to seek my happiness by limiting my desires, rather than in attempting to satisfy them."

JOHN STUART MILL

LIVING SLOWLY ALLOWS you to consume less, but it goes the other direction, too. Consuming less allows you to live more slowly. Slow livers need to address consumption with honesty and a heightened sense of self-knowledge.

To live more slowly, you might need to find more time to self-actualize. Some people prefer to work less than full-time in order to focus more intentionally on people and experience-making. Working less might necessitate learning how to live happily on less money, which is so much easier than you think. It requires that you reframe what you really want. If you genuinely want less, you do not feel deprived.

One method of learning to want less is to understand what your *actual needs* entail. Make a list of ten *actual needs* here:

1.

2.

3.

4.

5.

6.

7.

8.

9.

10.

Now, make a list of ten of your _perceived_ or _manufactured_ needs.
These are items that you are brainwashed to believe that you need because of our vulnerability to marketing, friends, media, magazines... Frankly, these may be 'wants'.

1.

2.

3.

4.

5.

6.

7.

8.

9.

10.

Chances are that you will find that your _actual needs_ include some of the following; to nourish your body with food, to protect yourself with clothing, to shelter your body, to stimulate your intellect, to shower gifts on others, to surround yourself with beauty. If you have a family, these needs will extend to providing these for others, too. There is a great continuum within each of these categories that provides so much room for liberating yourself.

For each category of needs, you can explore either end of the continuum. Take for example the need to nourish your body with food. You can choose to consume inexpensive homegrown and home-made food. On the other end of the continuum, you can go to fancy restaurants several times a week. With clothing, there is a great deal of ground between Salvation Army and Saks. You can entertain yourself with free concerts, public spaces and lectures or you can choose pricier ways to stimulate yourself. You can buy birthday and Christmas gifts for others that are lavish (the latest gadget, jewelry that will rarely be used) or you can craft your own jewelry, scarves, mittens. You can always convey a lovely sentiment just by creating your own heartfelt notecards or clipping an article that reminds you of them.

By choosing to meet your needs with less expense, you buy your own freedom. Only you know where you are comfortable with changing your behaviors, so this discernment must be a highly individualized process of reorganizing priorities. Remember though: the less you need, the more freedom you have.

The first noble truth of the Buddha is that all life is suffering. The second noble truth is that suffering is actually the product of attachment. How painful it is to WANT, until, of course, that wanting is fulfilled and there is momentary happiness. This happiness lasts only until the next wanting begins. Freedom from want is freedom from attachment—the greatest cause of suffering. Therefore, freedom from want is a great step toward freedom from suffering. Of course, the first noble truth of Janis Joplin is that, "freedom's just another word for nothing left to lose."

Decades ago, Duane Elgin wrote the book, *Voluntary Simplicity.* This philosophy grew out of the concept of Voluntary Poverty that is often adopted by religious communities. You need not become an ascetic (one who renounces their body and all worldly things) in order to live slowly, but slow livers just don't need as many material possessions because they readily find satisfaction in the ones they have and the non-material parts of life. There is less desire to trade up on purses, houses, shoes, schools, zip codes and vacations.

Once you recognize that your actual needs are far more basic than your perceived needs, you will begin wanting less. You will find portions at restaurants to be absurd. You might even find it surreal when a friend is a slave to a job they hate in order to make the mortgage payments on a McMansion that is exorbitantly expensive and often just too big to even tastefully decorate.

This move toward decreasing your consumption must come from a joy in the lightness of having and wanting less. If you attempt to motivate your consumption behavior using the negative approach of deprivation, you will fail. For every act that feels like deprivation, there will be a corresponding binge. For every act of martyrdom, you will go off the rails. You need to be excited about moving toward this freer, less cluttered place where your footprint barely leaves a mark.

Personally, the prospect of living within a budget makes me cranky. However, I can get very enthusiastic about putting less crap into landfills. Find your positive motivation and move toward it. Maybe you like having less junk in your basement. Maybe you like a half-full closet. Maybe you think keeping your car for ten years is preferable to it becoming a heap of scrap metal. Maybe you just like the idea of watching a growing savings account. But, be keenly aware of whether or not budgets work for you or against you. For example, every time I have put myself on a STRICT BUDGET, it has spurred a gluttonous, unnecessary spending binge which results in an incurable consumption hangover that lasts for weeks.

Wanting Less is catching on. Two years ago I learned about a movement called *"The Compact,"* where signers commit to not buy any new item for a full year. The premise of the Compact was to try to slow the filling of landfills, but it was also an exercise for 'compacters' to learn how to live with less. It's a challenge, and I couldn't do it—especially with small children. It is a great exercise and means of self-examination. Look at the **http://sfcompact.blogspot.com** for a beautiful description of what a small group of individuals are trying to accomplish. Here is their creed:

The Compact

❶ to go beyond recycling in trying to counteract the negative global environmental and socioeconomic impacts of U.S.. consumer culture, to resist global corporatism, and to support local businesses, farms, etc;

❷ to reduce clutter and waste in our homes (as in trash compact-er);

❸ to simplify our lives (as in calm-pact)

Freecycling is almost as common as new convention centers in most cities now. This is the slang term for recycling by giving away an item for free. In our city, Freecycle stands are set up at various outdoor markets. My arty friends have always worn thrift clothes, but now I see that my mother's friends are even venturing out to consignment shops. The more people are freecycling and recycling clothes, furniture, cars and stuff, the more socially acceptable it will become. One person's junk is another person's treasure.

You might not be the type that can embrace thrift clothing or buy a used car. This might give you the willies or require more humility than you can muster. Don't beat yourself up for loving the finer, newer things in life. You can have them, just have fewer of them. The key with minimizing and slowing your consumption is to be crystal clear about exactly what you 'need' and what will truly satisfy you in order to reduce buyer's regret and overconsumption. If you have a keen sense of your body type, your wardrobe gaps and your sense of style, you will hone your ability to make mostly perfect purchases.

In the area of entertainment, if you have thoroughly examined *what you love* and *what you can live without,* you will develop the ability to buy only theatre tickets, music and vacations that are closer to the bullseye, with a higher success rate. Research to find out if 1) you can get it free somehow, 2) the reviews are excellent and from respected sources, 3) you can rent it. It is always a good idea to mull over a major purchase just to be certain that you really feel you need it. You won't find yourself making mistakes and thinking the day after,

"Why did I go there/buy that/eat that? What a waste of money/time/energy."

Portion control only works for me if the quality meets my high expectations. I can savor the small wardrobe/jewelry/art collection/house/meal only if it is extremely satisfying. If you end up buying something that isn't quite right, you may be dissatisfied and then you will go on a consumption rampage chasing a taste. A good example of lousy portion control is this: I had an *actual need*. I needed a place to sit in my living room. My instincts told me that I wanted to fill that need with this one special couch. I knew it would be perfect in my house, in my life, with my décor, and that its quality was so good that I could be buried with it. I knew this because I had a deep knowledge of my style, having played 'interior designer' for my friends and family for years. But, I didn't feel like I should spend the money. I ended up buying THREE not-quite-right but less expensive couches over the course of fifteen years in an attempt to NOT buy the ONE couch I really knew was my soulmate.

This was a significant lesson learned. I found out the hard way about the importance of Sustainable Style. I tired of chasing around and finally bought 'the' couch about five years ago. I'm satisfied and haven't thought once about this since. It no longer occupies brain power or shopping energy. In order to want less, you need to do your research, know exactly what you want and try to get it right the first time. Keen self-knowledge allows you to spend less time chasing a taste.

Sometimes, we consume to fill empty spaces. We like to have new things because we want something to talk about. It could be that having the latest toy or car or purse makes us feel slightly more powerful, advanced, smart or sexy. Maybe you think that a new house will make you less lonely or more happy? It's so important that we examine the underlying reason we think we need to consume. Don't judge it when you find the answer. There is a valid reason you want what you want. Just bring it out into the light. Cajole it like it's a scared dog cowering under a bed. Tell it you aren't going to criticize it. It is what it is. But, now that you know why you wanted that thing you don't need, just be awake to it. Waking up to our rationales can help wear them away. They lose their fake power. Maybe that dress isn't going to make me look skinny, after all. Maybe that zip code won't make me feel like a success. Just see it for what it is and be compassionate with your demons.

"Manufactured Need" is terribly seductive with ingenious marketing to work us into a frenzy about every new toy, piece of technology, style of clothing and hip new restaurant. If you can try to curtail your intake of marketing of Manufactured Need, you will lose some of your desire to possess the latest thing. To adapt a cliché, 'you are what you consume.' Try to allow fewer ads into your system and you will feel less needy.

Consider the outside forces that fuel your desire for the latest, unnecessary thing. It's not just advertisements in the media, but it may be that certain people or places push your consumption buttons. Stores that are full of your favorite eye candy may be too much for you. Go less often. Buy, but buy less. Watch less television and listen to commercial free radio. Attempt to surround yourself with people who have also flipped conspicuous consumption on its head. There honestly are people who sit around and talk about how to diminish their footprint, repair their own clothes and downsize to a smaller, high-density house. They are usually nice, too.

Another tip for Wanting Less is that greed and gluttony don't seem to grow in a grateful heart. Making a list of what you are grateful for every day is a smart way of making your life feel sufficiently full already. Before you decide that you need something, take an appreciative inventory of what you already have that might fit the bill.

Beauty

*"We live only to discover beauty.
All else is a form of waiting."*

KAHLIL GIBRAN

THINK OF SOMETHING you consider beautiful and loll it around in your brain as if it were a piece of hard candy. It should take at least five minutes to suck all the flavor out of that thought.

Heavy silk tapestry?

A pale pink dogwood tree?

Ornate sterling silver flatware?

An Andrew Wyeth painting?

That one chord that stirs you from inside every time?

Children playing in an Italianate fountain?

A well-ironed, crisp white shirt?

Beautifully painted crown molding?

A well-manicured lawn?

Kim Novak?

These things feed us. We should be metaphorically eating them and getting them into our bloodstream with as much regularity as is possible. There are zero calories and no threat of adverse consequences, and much of it is free. We can consume it, let it flow through our system and permanently improve us. Beauty takes away loneliness, hunger, sadness and anxiety. Beauty replaces our imbalance with peace, goodwill, happiness, calm, energy and love.

Beauty is one of the missing links in America today. We seem to have forgotten its importance. Are we scrambling furiously, trying to backfill our need for beauty but we have forgotten how? Because we don't recognize what we are chasing, we are attempting to fill this void with food, materialism, television, technology and cheap surrogates for beauty. Don't do this to yourself. Recognize that you need to have drop dead gorgeous beauty in your life as much as you need Potassium. Find the beauty that feeds you well and then let it restore you.

Have you ever experienced a Fellini film? I love mid-century European film because of its unapologetic obsession with beauty. These films illustrate a broad based cultural adoration of beauty through the luxurious fabrics, the tailor-made clothing, the land-scaped public gardens, the ornate fountains, the well-coiffed women, the snappily dressed men and the beautiful food. It's delicious. Brace yourself, however, because Fellini gives us a stark foil against which to compare today's standards of American beauty.

A personal love affair with beauty is healthy in feeding our senses and helping us feel satisfaction. Beauty is available to anyone who is willing to put on the figurative glasses that will permit you to see beauty. It's available to you in public parks. It's in the vegetable you are about to eat, the public sculpture, the children walking down the street, the yoga pose, the foam in your cappuccino. Let it wash away the mediocrity of strip mall architecture and ill-fitting sweatpants. You can put on these glasses more readily by wearing them often. In *The Artist's Way,* Julia Cameron talks at length about 'artist dates.' For your own artist's date, take yourself out every week to enjoy works of tactile and visual beauty. This practice attunes you to noticing the beauty that already exists. It hones your ability to see it more readily. I am a regular at the fabric, wallpaper, tile, granite stores. I don't buy anything, but I touch almost everything. A friend of mine takes daily hikes through the county park and reports back on the shades of the leaves. My father watches wildlife (yes, he holds a gun so he can be manly, but he really just watches the deer). Practice this often so that you can nurture an intimate relationship with beauty.

I wonder how we could attempt to reignite passion for beauty in America? Finding, creating and satiating our need for beauty requires time and attention. Whether taking an interest in your own fashion, designing and caring for a beautiful garden, improving the public market with bright paint and window boxes or serving as a volunteer for a local arts organization, these all take time. All of these tiny bits of beauty are rewarded with a smile from the community and from yourself.

It is pleasing to both the individual who creates the beauty, but also to the strangers who appreciate the work. It would be transformative to individuals and society if we created a culture of both producing and consuming beauty. If we did, how would we be different? Would people have more pride? Would people be happier? Would people be friendlier? Are people more open to living fully when they are creating or appreciating beauty? We can start by appreciating what is already lovely. We can proceed by beautifying what isn't.

Can you fully appreciate beauty if you are moving too fast? No. It's impossible to be awake to beauty if you are being distracted. Can you fully enjoy a museum, a concert, your garden, making love, the scent of a stranger's perfume? No, you actually need to move slowly in order to enjoy every drop of nectar. If you are moving too fast, you will miss the tantalizing vital parts of living.

Speed often gives birth to sloppiness (fast food, a flawed business model or a bad haircut). However, if you devote attention, time and loving kindness to any activity, it is almost impossible to create horrible results.

Ask yourself the following;

Where can I begin appreciating beauty?

How can I create more beauty in my life?

How can I plant the seed of a culture of beauty in my community?

When does beauty help me consume less?

Empty Spaces

"An empty canvas is a living wonder...
far lovelier than certain pictures."

WASSILY KANDINSKY

MY DAUGHTER, FROM ABOUT AGE TWO, would crawl into her crib every once in a while. I thought it was odd, but our Great Aunt considered her to be enlightened. She said, "Look, she knows when she needs a break!" As parents, most of us try to ensure that our little ones have free time after a play date or pre-school to unwind and decompress. Teachers know that school-age kids can't retain a thing if they don't have their recess. Since we as adults don't have parents and teachers orchestrating our empty spaces, we must learn to notice when we need to insert a truly empty break.

Empty space for thoughts

Free-range animals seem to be all the rage right now. My meat-eating friends tell me that animals are a great deal happier and healthier if they have wide spaces in which to roam. Our thoughts are like that. The greatest epiphanies can't be nurtured in chicken battery cages; one on top of the other crammed into a square foot space with other thoughts squawking above and below on either side. Our best revelations occur during or often after walks, meditation, gardening, showers –when they've had plenty of space to roam.

Protecting these empty spaces is critical. Even when I was living fast and furious, I used to walk alone for an hour a few times a week for exercise. It was then that I had my best ideas for work. After I got my ipod and fell in love with podcasts, I stopped having break-through ideas at my job. My brain needed the emptiness in order to leap forward.

Be grateful, too, for the informal empty spaces when they occur unexpectedly. You can transform the frustration of a traffic jam or a late appointment by reframing. You are, in fact, exceptionally lucky to have a bit of free time! Another example is this: your doctor is running behind schedule and you are forced to sit in the waiting area. You can either choose to A) enjoy the newfound free time or B) get angry. The end result if you choose option A is peace. The outcome of option B is wrinkles and high blood pressure. Knowing the ultimate impact, why wouldn't you train yourself to look for the silver lining in unexpected empty spaces?

Empty spaces can heighten our when we are being and not doing. (Recall that we are human beings, not human doings.) It's when I'm walking through the garden that I hear the music in the rustle of the leaves. The snowflakes are never more magical than when I am drinking tea and looking out the window. The neighborhood smells of families cooking dinner delight me on evening walks through my city. Paying attention to your senses during empty spaces helps you fully appreciate even small gifts.

These empty spaces are golden moments, where epiphanies occur which guide us with our careers and relationships. Don't destroy them by chronically checking your Blackberry! It may be necessary to designate some time every day where you sit quietly and unplug entirely. Meditation, walking, knitting, painting, vacuuming, ironing, weeding might not be entirely 'empty' spaces, but as long as you aren't multi-tasking, they give your free-range spirit space to roam. Give yourself permission to not 'do' for some time each day. Come to recognize the value of the empty space so that you will want to protect and nurture these spaces.

Empty spaces for our bodies

Physical empty spaces include places that are free from much décor, noise or motion. These can be parks, fields, empty stadiums, forests, sidewalks, bike paths, rivers, oceans, cemeteries or even deserted industrial parks. It can also be your office. One can also choose to decorate in a manner that minimizes visual stimulation. These physical empty spaces encourage you to breathe freer and decompress.

While this prescription for living slowly smacks of Transcendentalism, I am not advocating that you go build a house in the woods. City dwelling is a far greener thing you can do for the earth. Unwind yourself in parks, playgrounds, even cemeteries in your existing community or go out to a public green space in the country. We can be Urban Transcendentalists. If everyone chooses to buy up an acre of woods or farmland, there eventually won't be any open spaces left. Enjoy the vast empty spaces, but leave only footprints.

Fleshy Social Capital

*"There is a communion of more than bodies when bread
is broken and wine is drunk."*

MFK FISCHER

I HAVE MIXED FEELINGS about social capital. In general, in the abstract, *especially* in fiction, social capital is breathtakingly heartwarming. On paper and in the lecture halls, there is nothing more exhilarating than being swept away in the momentum of vibrant social connectivity. This is evidenced by the fact that there is likely no quote more often cited than Margaret Mead's "A small group of thoughtful people could change the world. Indeed, it's the only thing that ever has."

As with anything so seductive, we humans need rules. Social capital must be embraced hand in glove with the concept of healthy boundaries. Also, we are fleshy for a reason and I think our socializing should mostly occur in the flesh. I think we need to touch, smell, see, taste and hear each other. I've logged millions of hours participating in both virtual social capital and non-virtual (in the flesh) social capital. It is my unempirical but wholehearted belief that we actually NEED the fleshy kind. This fleshy kind feeds us in a deeper way than the virtual kind. I have no data to prove this. Try it for yourself. Use only your personal experiences as the judge and jury.

For many people, especially those who are extroverted and obtain energy from being around great piles of other people, social capital of any type is essential. If they aren't actually working with others, socializing, interfacing or networking, they are hungry for it. I have neighbors like this. They are the saints that organize our community garden, coordinate the neighborhood bike race and host potlucks on Sundays. I consider myself blessed to be in their pack. These are the people that Robert Putnum might wish to live on every block. Heck, I want them on every block!

Regardless of your ideal portion of social capital, I would encourage you to choose the fleshy over the virtual kind as much as possible. I have learned through trial and error that I do not require more than a tablespoon of this ingredient, however, that small portion must be a sensory-rich, short, deep, authentic and intense connection.

Think about a period in your life when you felt really balanced. What was your social life like then?

What sort of connecting do you need to feel balanced?

Is that sustainable in the long-term? Why or why not?

Consider whether or not you prefer formal (boards, volunteering, church) or informal (coffee house, picnics, cocktail parties) social capital. A mix of both? Neither? Know yourself.

As I was writing this chapter at Chestnut Hill Café, three people sitting at the coffee bar started talking about Irish music and loudly singing obscure songs together. After about a half an hour of watching these people enjoy each other, the tallest one stood up, pushed back from his chair and said, "Well, it was great meeting all of you. My name is Ed."

I was shocked to learn they weren't old friends! They all shook fleshy hands, smiled, laughed in unison and went their separate ways. They touched each other in a way that gave them real happiness. They will probably continue coming back to Chestnut Hill for another cup of sweet humanity.

This happened because they were all three open to it. They didn't have earbuds in. Unlike me, they were not pecking away at their laptop. They were open-hearted, wide awake and *expecting* good people to fall into their laps.

Diffusing Narcissism

Narcissus was the son of a Greek god. After a spell was cast on him, he looked at his reflection in a pond one day and fell wildly in love. He stayed there and looked at himself in the pond for the rest of his life.

SELF-LOVE IS A GOOD THING; but not when it becomes all-consuming. Self-love can easily become addictive. How quickly we lose the ability to look up from the pond (or screen). Narcissism feeds the vanity, materialism, careerism and lousy relationships that are contributing factors of a too-fast life. When we learn to defuse our own narcissism and others' overblown egos, we can live more intentionally. Only once we look up from the pond can we authentically focus on those priorities in life which matter to us in the longview.

I have discovered a few means of counteracting narcissism which grows in oneself and in others. Be vigilant in diagnosing this virus and compassionate in treating the patients.

Separate the narcissism from the true self

One method to begin defusing narcissism is by simply recognizing it for what it is. Whether it is your own demon or someone else's, pull it out into the light and see that this overactive ego is NOT the true self. When you encounter a self-absorbed person, see this as their false self. Look for their true self underneath the bluster. Try to see that person (even if it's YOU!) with compassion. No one wants to be self-obsessed, but they slip into it and need help finding their way back to humility. Just bringing it into the light with loving-kindness and separating it from the person will improve the situation.

Love 'em through it

When I was in my twenties, I worked at a nonprofit in Baltimore where people living with end-stage AIDS came to live for a short while before they died. The Program Director, Dorris, was a wise southern

Episcopalian who wore lots of flax and would 'supervise' us on long contemplative walks. You knew you had really screwed up if she took you out for a beer after your walk.

As happens with young idealistic do-gooders, regularly one of us would become enthralled by our reflection in the pond. When these ego situations would flummox the rest of the team, we'd take our concerns to Dorris. She would listen to us whine for about a half an hour during a staff meeting and then she would put down her knitting, look up, smile and drawl, "Well, looks like we're just gonna have to love 'em through it." And then, as an exclamation point with a smiley face on it, she would burst out laughing. So, we learned to love 'em through it. After a month or two, the egomaniac offender would wake up from their trance and announce at the dinner table, "Boy, was I ever being an asshole."

You really can take the poison out of narcissism by compassionately loving the jerk, even if you're the jerk. Both St. Therese's Little Way and Tonglen meditation from Tibetan Buddhism are powerful tools for reversing the narcissism. Both help me to use imperfection (including narcissism) as FUEL for creating good. It's loosely analogous to converting the methane gas from cow poop into electricity. You take in the bad, purify it, and then put it back into the world in a constructive way.

The little way
Saint Therese of Lisieux figured out how to turn lemons into lemonade at a very young age. St. Therese felt strongly that we are to love one another. She wanted to learn how to love flawed people, too. She figured out how to love the jerks with the most perfect kind of love she could muster. She wrote, "I realise now, that perfect love means putting up with other people's shortcomings, feeling no surprise at their weaknesses, finding encouragement even in the slightest evidence of good qualities in them."

Therese needed to find a way to prove her love through action and she recognized that it is through the smallest actions that she could love the greatest. Therese wrote, "That shall be my life, to scatter flowers—to miss no single opportunity of making some small sacrifice, here by a smiling look, there by a kindly word, always doing the tiniest things right, and doing it for love." She found that when she would deny her own self-will so that she could offer a little kindness, she was really able to love imperfect people with a more perfect love.

Tonglen

Tonglen is a Tibetan Buddhist form of meditation that translates as giving and taking or sending and taking. In this form of meditation, one visualizes taking in the suffering of others and then giving one's own happiness to others. It's sort of an exchange, or a cleaning of bad into good.

Tonglen, like The Little Way, works wonders in reducing narcissism in both yourself and in others. It also develops a heightened sense of loving kindness.

Tonglen requires a strong spirit in order to take on the suffering of others. You should learn more about this practice before you start. It's notable, however, that many people (myself included) began using this method of breathing in the bad and exhaling out clearly directed good, long before I ever knew it was a formal meditation technique. I wonder if it is in our nature to help others this way? Expect to be blown away by results.

Forgiveness

My kids go to a Catholic Elementary School, even though I'm not Catholic. One day I went to volunteer for playground duty. I happened to be fuming about an injustice that I had just experienced. I was practically growling, puffing up like a bear and completely forgetting everything I've written about in this chapter. I walked up the steps of the school and there, taped to the front door in large choppy construction paper were seven letters "F O R G I V E".

Are you grateful for the forgiveness from someone who had the grace to overlook your flaws? Your parents? Your partner? Your children? Especially your children?!? Your dog? An employee? A friend?

They love us in spite of the fact that we really suck sometimes. My very forgiving yoga instructor told me that forgiving others is the most selfish thing I could do. She was right. It's true. Who are you going to experiment with forgiving now, even if they don't deserve it?

Live/Work/Play

THE IDEA OF LIVE/WORK/PLAY popped out of the community development efforts in Maryland in the mid 1990s. I was actually living in the first neighborhood in Baltimore that espoused this philosophy wherein you live close to everything you need. It made sense as a means of saving older neighborhoods and combating urban sprawl. Live/work/play fostered a personal place-based intimacy with the place and the people that I hadn't experienced since I was growing up in Shaker Heights, a renowned neighborhood in Cleveland. Live/work/play nurtures a sense of joyous, squeaky clean neighborhood pride. I literally adored my neighborhood in Baltimore. Live/work/play gave me permission to be an eco-Mr. Rogers finding passion and gritty writing material in the people in my neighborhood.

The concept is also helpful in that non-committal relationship kind of way. In your daily routine, you become friendly with the shopkeepers, market stand-holders, politicians, neighbors and police. You may live close to your kids' teachers or your co-workers. There is power in this incidental networking with people from various socio-economic castes. Over repeated interactions with strangers, you eventually feel that you know them, even though you don't. One day you might even feel compelled to ask how their new baby is, hold open a door, fluff up their dog's ears or push their car out of the snow. So too, you become more cognizant about properly picking up your dog's poop and the final resting place of your gum. These little bits of neighborliness are the golden links that strengthen a civilized society. They appear small, but they build solidarity and pride in our communities while we practice respecting people from varied walks of life.

If you practice Live/Work/Play, you will find that you develop a joyful commitment to that place to keep it safe, clean, friendly and nurturing. Even a misanthrope may find themselves feeling intangible community pride.

There are also obvious health benefits of walking/biking to work/ errands. Academics are now studying the health benefits of a live/ work/play lifestyle.

There are economic benefits to living close to your work and play, too. Consider the financial benefits of not having to have two cars, a gas budget, a long commute, car insurance, coming home for lunch and arriving home earlier from work. Add it up!

Finally, if you have a tendency toward pessimism, it's amazing how optimizing these 'sidewalk relationships' can be. You have to allow yourself to be open to them, but a simple backyard chat can turn your frown upside down. No one more than stay-at-home-moms knows the miraculous effect of amiable strangers on the playground at the community park. A few sentences can elevate you from the depths of depression to happiness. It's a natural gift we humans can give to each other and it makes a lot of sense. Live/Work/Play in one community. Be one of the fibers in the blanket.

Move Mindfully

SINCE LIVING SLOWLY REQUIRES you to be in touch with your senses as much as possible, it is essential to find means of connecting your body to your mind. The more you work these two in concert, the more you can appreciate living simply and find satisfaction in small portions. You can only maximize your absorption of whatever you are consuming if your mind is fully registering the experience. The more you can connect your body and mind, the less excess you desire—emotionally and materially. It's a wise investment to find means of optimizing the relationship between your mind and body. I was awestruck the first time I ate good chocolate while I was fully conscious. I was finished after two squares. If you are connected and paying attention, a vintage la Perla nightgown will please you more than an entire semi-conscious trip to Italy.

There are many tools for enhancing this level of awareness by connecting your mind and body, but the ones I find to be most accessible are walking and yoga.

Walking is probably the most common way of connecting the mind and body, but you have to encourage the connection to occur. If you opt to walk in silence, without earbuds to muddle up the works, you give your brain and body a much-needed chance to reconnect. This declutters unnecessary and unhealthy thinking. Simple walking clarifies you: the lightbulb will turn on. You can find the right word or the ideal solution to a problem. Moving your body by walking removes sticky clots that gum up your brain. See if it works for you. You may want to vary where you walk to see if the results vary, too. Find out how and where walking works for you.

Yoga also connects your full self. Don't be overwhelmed by the myriad types of yoga offerings. Think of them as ice cream flavors and sample them over time. Discover what works for you. Hatha Yoga is designed to do this reconnecting. It's been an amazing catalyst of remarkable epiphanies in my life. Not only am I aware of my body in a way that I hadn't been before, but I've learned about intimacy from yoga. Yoga has helped me see how many layers there are to my life, and that I had only been scratching the surface when I was living too fast. Yoga is a tried and true method of removing brain goo. Trust it.

Longviewing

"I am tomorrow, or some future day, what I establish today. I am today what I established yesterday or some previous day."

JAMES JOYCE

LONGVIEWING IS PROBABLY THE SIMPLEST INGREDIENT but most difficult to include in your recipe.

If, before pursuing an activity, taking a job, beginning a relationship, eating something, you consider the LONGVIEW, you might just make a different choice. Consider the longview. You can determine how long, but it should be farther out than the short-term. This counteracts the desire for immediacy.

Consider how this works in your daily decision-making. I usually think about a ten year span into the future as my longview. Determine a number of years/months/minutes that is your longview period of time.

Who would you be friends with if you considered the longview?

Who wouldn't you be friends with if you considered the longview?

What job would you have if you considered the longview?

What activities would you pursue if you considered the longview?

What activities wouldn't you pursue if you considered the longview?

Here are some big and little changes I owe to longviewing:

- Wear sunscreen
- Always be honest
- Smile at strangers
- Never smoke
- Drink less
- Quit destructive jobs or people
- Sleep more
- Read books more
- Read the newspaper less
- But read the Sunday NY Times more
- Say NO more often
- Follow my bliss more
- Stretch
- Listen to old people
- Clean my gutters
- Follow my instincts
- Apologize

Taking the longview aids in slowing one's life by eliminating distractions, short-sighted mistakes and white noise.

Uni-tasking

DO ONE THING AT A TIME. It's the opposite of multi-tasking.

Uni-tasking allows you to remember what you've just done. You experience life more fully. You taste your food, enjoy your friend and feel your body. When you are on the phone, listen to the speaker. When you walk your dog, be part of the experience. When you check your email, really read the words that the writer spent time crafting.

In addition to being happier, you won't lose your keys so much anymore. People will think you are a gift because you are actually paying attention to them. This is a rare and precious occurrence and they will feel better after spending time with you. They will think you are enlightened and kind just because you are doing one thing intentionally. They will be right!

5

Alphabet of Slow Origins

"I pretended to be somebody I wanted to be until finally I became that person. Or he became me."

CARY GRANT

WORDS ARE POWERFUL. The stories we tell ourselves need to be well-crafted so that we can craft artisanal lives. Infuse more of these words into your daily rotation and see what happens.

Balance	Dinner party	Hear
Balcony	Discipline	Intentional
Beauty	Eccentric	Interests
Bike	Empty space	Intimacy
Calm	Enjoy	Joy
Canoe	Equilibrium	Kindnesses
Civilized	Family	Laughter
Community	Focus	Less
Concern	Forgiveness	Lessons learned
Connect	Friendship	Listen
Cook	Gratitude	Long-term
Deck	Grow	Longview

Love

Mature

Meditate

Neighbor

Park

Passion

Peace

Place

Porch

Pray

Privacy

Public benefit

Sacrifice

Satisfaction

Savor

Scent

Sensual

Sidewalk

Silence

Silly

Slow

Small

Soft

Solitude

Stop

Sustainable

Taste

Think

Thought

Thoughtful

Touch

Uni-tasking

Us

Walk

Appendix

Resources that informed this book

Bowling Alone, Dr. Robert Putnum

Bread for the Journey, Henry Nowen

Concord, Massachusetts, the Fertile Crescent of Living Slowly

Feeding the Hungry Heart, Geneen Roth

Getting to Yes, Roger Fisher and William Ury

Green Urbanism, Timothy Beatley

The film *I HEART Huckabees,* directed by David O. Russell

In Praise of Slowness, Carol Honore

Learning to Love You More, Harrell Fletcher and Miranda July

The film *Lost in Translation,* directed by Sofia Coppola

No One Belongs Here More Than You, Miranda July

Peace is Every Step, Thich Nhat Hanh

Positive No, William Ury

Siblings Without Rivalry, Adele Faber and Elaine Mazlish

Story of a Soul, St. Therese of Lisieux

Taking Sustainable Cities Seriously, Kent Portney

The Art of Eating, MFK Fischer

The Death and Life of Great American Cities, Jane Jacobs

The End of Nature, Bill McKibben

The Geography of Bliss, Eric Weiner

The Impossible Will Take a Little While, Paul Rogat Loeb (editor)

The Key to Sustainable Cities, Gwendlyn Hallsmith

The Not So Big House, Sarah Susanka

The Power of a Positive No, William Ury

The Power of Appreciative Inquiry, Diana Whitney and Amanda Trosten-Bloom

The Rise of the Creative Class, Richard Florida

The film *The Royal Tennenbaums,* directed by Wes Anderson

The Slow Food Movement

The Small-mart Revolution, Michael Shuman

The Social Life of Small Urban Spaces, William Holly Whyte

The Spirit of Community, Amitai Etzioni

The Square, Marguerite Duras

Thomas-Kilmann Conflict Instrument

Voluntary Simplicity, Duane Elgin

Walden, Henry David Thoreau

World Changing: A User's Guide for the 21st Century, Alex Steffen

www.hypomanicedge.com

www.slowmovement.com

Zen Flesh, Zen Bones, Paul Reps and Nyogen Senzaki

Made in the USA
Coppell, TX
29 July 2021